Come to Power

*Eleven
Contemporary
American Indian Poets*

Edited by Dick Lourie

*with
an introduction
by Joseph Bruchac*

*The
Crossing Press
Trumansburg
New York*

ACKNOWLEDGMENTS

Some of these poems have appeared in the following magazines:
*The Phoenix, South Dakota Review, Hanging Loose, Northeast,
Spring Rain, Guabi, Galley Sail Review.*

"Old Tillicum" and "After the Death of an Elder Klallam,"
both in slightly different versions, first appeared in Duane Niatum's
book also titled *After The Death Of An Elder Klallam* (Baleen
Press, Phoenix, Arizona).

Joseph Bruchac's poems first appeared in his book *Indian
Mountain* (Ithaca House, Ithaca, New York).

Two of Minerva Allen's poems first appeared in her chapbook
One (Wopapi Press, Oakland, California).

Some of Karoniaktatie's poems are from a book, *Native Colours,*
being published by Akwesasne Notes (Akwesasne, Mohawk Nation,
via Rooseveltown, New York).

Design—David Sykes

SBN 0-912278-44-7 *(paper)*
SBN 0-912278-45-5 *(cloth)*
L.C. No. 73-86673

The Crossing Press Series of Contemporary Anthologies

Copyright The Crossing Press, 1974

CONTENTS:

THE CONNECTIONS

An Introduction

The other day I received a letter from Simon Ortiz. Simon spoke in it of a book I had sent him of poems by Kofi Awoonor, a Ghanian poet. The words Simon had to say were beautiful and appropriate:

> *"He's one of the best," Simon said, "a patient, humorous man. These are the true points of a tribal man, patience and humor. That lasting voice comes from a truly tribal person. He knows the connections or at the very least gives them recognition and respect. He realizes the timbre of the connections. He has to, because if he does not, things will separate and stop; his life will stop."*

The poems in this book are by people who have recognized and respected the connections. They have done so because their backgrounds have taught them that Earth is a mother and the world does not exist to be *used* or played with, but to be loved and respected as you love and respect your own body; or perhaps (for I do not know everyone in this book personally) because, like myself, they have rediscovered the value of ways which were a part of their blood if not their upbringing.

The variety of writing in *Come To Power* is considerable. Some of the poems could have been written just as easily 400 years ago as songs or stories. Norman Russell's "singing wolf speaks," Winston Mason's "The Raven" and Minerva Allen's "Dog Soldier renounced life" have that quality about them. If they were written in an Indian language an anthropologist might be studying those poems right now.

Some of these poems could not have been written in any time but this one. Lew Blockcolski's picture of "the 5 year Indian" is classic, especially these days when non-Indians have been used to infiltrate the American Indian Movement as spies for the Feds. Its humor is more gentle, but it reminds me of one of Don L. Lee's portraits of a black super-revolutionary who disappears when the heat is on.

Thinking of Black poetry, why don't Indians write the way militant Black writers do? I won't pass judgment on militant Black writers but simply say the Indian vision is very different. Leslie Silko said to me once, "My writing is a gift to the Earth." And she meant this with great humility. Her tale "A Geronimo Story" is that kind of gift, a beautifully crafted, wry true picture of the Indian confronted by the military mind, the Western mind. Her Laguna scouts have been badly treated by a Major (whose name is Littlecock, a great piece of dry humor) who has called them in because he is sure Geronimo is nearby and about to attack. Geronimo is not within 200 miles, but the Major will not listen to them. As the men walk back to their horses, Siteye, the old man, says:

> "I am only sorry that the Apaches aren't around
> here. I can't think of a better place to wipe out.
> If we see them tomorrow, we'll tell them to come
> here first."

Siteye's philosophy, "Anybody can act violently—there is nothing to it; but not every person is able to destroy his enemy with words." exemplifies the subtle American Indian sense of humor, a humor so subtle that most white men never knew what hit them including (if my friends will forgive me for mentioning them twice in one short introduction) many anthropologists.

Some of these poems present the picture of the shattered landscape of an America which the Indian has been forced to the very edges of. Suzan Shown's lovely poem which begins "i breathe as the night breathes..." contains the apocalyptic vision of:

> *blue eyes sons of fire*
> *they stand over me*
> *with yellow hair and white faces*
> *wearing laces made of rough skin*
> *of buffalo rotting in the sun*
> *near my village of now starved people*

S. Roberto Sandoval gives us a picture of something sacred defiled and hung up for tourists:

> *The*
> *pot's heart*
> *decorating a bell*
> *ceramic noise maker*
> *hanging in that shop*
> *tourist shop design*
> *pulled from the crook of*
> *dead man's arms...*

and Karoniaktatie tells us:

> *I have seen the material world*
> *I have tasted its bitter fruit*

Yet this bleakness is not all that there is. There is also celebration, a sense of new strength, things which come from the connections, from humor and patience and which can be felt so clearly in Leslie Silko's haunting "Slim Man Canyon."

There are only eleven writers in this book, but among them are some of the finest Indian poets we have today, young men and women who are giving their voices to the Earth and the human beings who live here. Duane Niatum, for example, is a voice which will last. His poem "Old Tillicum," in which I see my own grandfather, is one I have read many times and found new each time my eyes came to it. Ray Young Bear is another. His poems are so quiet, so very mysterious at times. There is a sense of something happening, of the voices of the land stirring to speak as in the first stanza of "Another Face:"

> *Small eyes water on the branch*
> *they have been there*
> *for a long time now*
> *thinking;*
> *please move your wings*
> *to show me I have found you*
> *at last.*

Yet the great thing, to me, is that this anthology, good as it is, only scratches the surface. There are people such as Phil George, Simon Ortiz, Grey Cohoe, James Welch, Wendy Rose, Harold Littlebird, Emerson Blackhorse Mitchell and many many more. They are out there, they are speaking and they are being heard. Anthologies such as this one make it more likely that more will want to hear them. For me, at least, a good anthology is always a reminder of how much more there is in store, like picking one berry at the edge of the woods and knowing from its taste that a whole summer full of berries is ahead.

Joseph Bruchac

PREFACE

I had read collections of traditional Indian songs and poetry, but had never seen an anthology of contemporary Indian poets. And both kinds seemed to me equally important, so I decided (about three years ago) to do this book.

We considered two titles for this collection: *Many Ways* and *Come To Power*. *Many Ways* is literal—I do not consider this book to be "representative" of anything. (I'm not sure any collection is ever representative of anything.) These eleven poets were chosen not because I see any trends, leanings, developments, etc.; but because, as I have implied above, I think it's time attention is paid to contemporary native people and their culture, and because, as a poet and editor, these are eleven poets whose work I like.

In the literary sense of school, trend, I was in fact happy to observe re-reading the whole manuscript that there's great diversity in style, a wide range of concerns and subjects, in short all sorts of things which will prevent scholars from drawing any general conclusions whatsoever.

The second title (which we finally chose) was *Come To Power*. I mean by that phrase an invocation which will have overtones religious, or political or cultural—any way a reader hears it in these poems.

I want to thank Simon Ortiz, Robert Bly, and Gary Snyder, who helped me contact some of the poets, and Walter Lowenfels, who gave me more addresses and a good deal of as they say encouragement and moral support.

Dick Lourie
Ithaca, New York

Suzan Shown

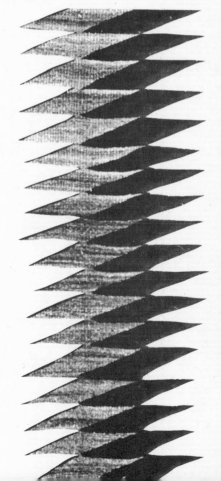

Suzan Shown lives in New York City where she works for the Pacifica Foundation's WBAI, a non-commercial listener-supported radio station. One of the programs she produces for the radio station is called Seeing Red, which deals with contemporary Indian concerns.

i breathe as the night breathes
i live as the forest life lives
the soft leaves and wet grass
are my protectors

above me in the clear night sea
are the torches of the gods
and the eyes of the dead
and the souls of the unborn
they surround my body with darkness
they give my shadowed mission
clear visioned sight
the night is my friend
      my heart's song is to the night

below me in the moist red earth
are the smooth round stones
and the bones of the dead
and the seeds of the unborn
the night worker worms beneath my body
remind me of the living worlds
giving morning birth
      my heart's song is to the earth

behind me in the sleep dead world
is Pipe Woman, my mother time
and Tall Man, my father earth
and Deer Eye, my sister dawn
the village sleepers stand beside my dream
giving comfort through the silent trials
of early rising suns
the sleeping ones are my friends
      my heart's song is to the sleeping ones

before me in the white blood world
are the blue eyed sons of fire
they stand over me
with yellow hair and white faces
wearing laces made of rough skins
of buffalo rotting in the sun
near my village of now starved people
wearing long braided black trophies
from the heads of my people
from the pride of my land

when the morning comes
i will continue to dream
and when i am killed
my soul will soar like the eagle
and from the great windy calm
i will dry the dawn tears
that blinded my sight
i will remember only the night
        my heart's song ends with the night

Ray Young Bear

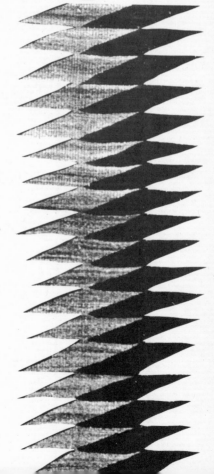

Ray Young Bear is a Mesquaki Indian from Tama, Iowa. He is a student at Grinnell College in Iowa and is majoring in art.

ANOTHER FACE

Small eyes water on the branch
they have been there
for a long time now
thinking:
please move your wings
to show me I have found you
at last.

* * *

this rock halfway out of the snow
turns away from the daylight
and cradles small blue footprints
into its stomach.
at night, they mark the snow again
keeping close to the rock.

WAR WALKING NEAR

death designs swirl high above faces that are of disbelief.
a captured people dressed in red hold hands and hum
to themselves a strange song.
brown rain slips fast into a sad freedom
low in the thoughts of the old man
who visioned the coming revolution.

he tells to his reflection a small word
not to reveal that in the night
he controls the night enemy
night-enemy-who-takes-us-with-magic-medicine.
he heard the eagle with eyes of war walking near.
they say the spring air comes without much intention.

THESE HORSES CAME

1.
from inside the bird a dream hums itself out and turns
into sky-wind rushing over my face that needs
a small feather from the otters nose to blow away
and create corners where i will stand
and think myself into hard ways.

2.
these horses came on light grey clouds
and carried off the barbed wire fence-post.
i started thinking about a divided bird
in four pieces of blood in winters hunt
with this certain song rolling the day westward.
the snow falls in one direction and loses me
as i breathe the whiteness like magic.

3.
the railroad tracks steal a distance
makes me forget which way
the eager crows are singing/low against the quiet.
in my dream-eye came her words and reminded
me of a story i once fell asleep to.

i aim my rifle cautiously at the sun
and ask: are you really afraid of children?

4 SONGS OF LIFE

1. a young man

the blue rain
quiet in feelings
losing
nothing—showing no one
that i am cold
in this
earth
singing different songs
i never heard
from the same people
unable
to
create or remember
their own
songs to keep.

2. an old man alone

i remember well
my people's
songs.
i will not reveal
to anyone
that i
know these songs.
it was
intended for me
to keep
them
in
secrecy
for they are now
mine to die with me.

3. one who realized

i sang
to the warm sun
and cold moon
this morning
and offered
myself
to the land
and gods
for them
to
teach
me
the old
hard ways
of living
all over again.

4. he was approached

a time
in sadness
within
the night
holding me
and comforting me.
here i am
being
taught
to be
a man
with life
and old sacred
songs to guide
me
and love me forever.

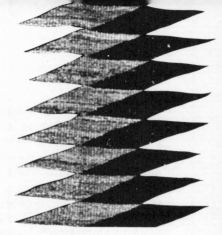

Lew Blockcolski

" . . . born in Enid, Oklahoma in 1943 of mixed blood parents. Father Cherokee, Mother Choctaw. Lived early years in what is now called low-income situation which allows for closer life to trees, flowers, streams etc. but not much contact with larger than three room houses, or diet of more than fried bread, beans and greens. Attended all the public schools, a church related university called Phillips University in Enid for a B.A. Also attended Wichita State University in Wichita, Kansas. One of those fairly-well-educated mixed breeds who works for the government because no great demand for us anywhere else."

THE 5 YEAR INDIAN

Frankie was a pony baby,
baptized without food bowls
or ceremony fires in a gold
defaced church near the reservation.
No feathers, no beads nor stains
adorned his head for twenty one years.
Five years ago, he was Mexico race,
so enrollment cards say,
Today with feathers flying,
hair growing, beads banding,
leather fringing and AIM card waving,
he is one of us.

LITTLE FEATHER SPEAKS

Mother married four times.
Grandmother said she
left me in a ditch on
the reservation Rock Road.

I was three weeks,
no four weeks old.
Now mother wants me back,
my Grandmother told me.

If I go back to her,
I am seven now,
she would not get me out
the door to any old ditch.

GEORGIA'S CHAMPION

Moving through shattered phoenix pottery,
the Cherokee outlet was stripped away
by froth covered mares in Peyote dreams
of Waukomis's white plains asylum.
A moon's death ahead of tribe decision
he rode out to reclaim Georgia.
But, somewhere on the trailless Interstate
Georgia lost another champion
in a rear end collision with
a moving company van.

TRANSLATION OF A PRAIRIE BAND POTTAWATOMI PRAYER

Ahau Mesek Mekkwe,
  (Welcome Mother Earth,)
bina bau doieg,
  (made clean by the rains)
andotmonk nijokmowiak gijuk
  (we ask you to help us grow among)
nebecknegen mickoyen min nebecknegen pugwen;
  (rotting weeds and rotting leaves;)
awi pitc begacukon cacga
  (so when the snows fall blinding you)
miziak kin geze munogmouk pok.
  (we can give ourselves to you in winter daylight.)

On the translation, the pronunciation is phonetic as the Pottawatomi symbols are nonexistent. That is about all one needs to know on that. The music is impossible for various reasons, the major being no one is allowed to record the music as the prayer is sung. The age of the prayer is difficult to determine except that it is not apparently a prayer of the Eastern Pottawatomi which the Prairie Band was once a part of. The Eastern Pottawatomi are located in Michigan and Wisconsin. The removal of the prairie group occurred in the 1830's. Therefore it is probably dated some time after that period. It is not presently in continuous use by the whole tribe and the faction which still uses it would rather not reveal anything about it.

POETRY

A quail leg wrenched in
two splintering pieces with sharp
saber points; pale meat hanging by
strings and black marrow pouring out,
waiting for the squaw's fire—that
is a poem to me—ugly enough to
disturb for understanding.

THE LIFE OF MAN

The power pole is crooked and crossed
in the evening sky.
Its transformer is dull metal
hung in suspension.
I want to run into the field
and cut it right down.
But Charlie Horse borrowed my axes yesterday.

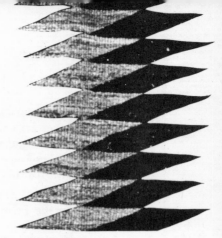

Norman Russell

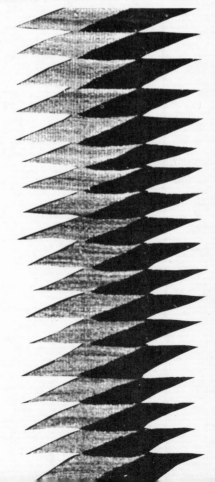

". . . That part of me which is Indian dominates that part of me which is European. It gives me a pride and a pleasure, and especially a wisdom, I could not find in cities, books, and universities, nor in all the written histories of America and Europe.

I was trained as an ecologist in the 1940's and this work has taken me into all parts of America, into hundreds of forests and prairies. Here I have seen degradation. And here I have listened, seen and felt the history of the Indian peoples. For tens of thousands of years they lived in deep harmony with the universe, and with God.

If you sense this harmony in my poems, then I begin to succeed in creating again for you an honesty and a worship that you may never have known—if you are white.

For, you see, you white men and women are utterly obsessed with death. The Indian was enthralled by, overcome with life. You walk before your god. The Indian walked with his god. You talk continually about love. The Indian loved. You have so far forgotten joy and beauty that you never mention them any more. The Indian found beauty and joy in every moment in every thing."

THE TREE SLEEPS IN THE WINTER

the tree sleeps in the winter he
moves where the wind wishes him he
returns and he nods his head like
the child in the afternoon but he
cannot lie down

does the tree think thoughts
in the winter does he remember
the summer does he stand in
the snow waiting can the tree wait
as i wait?

do the trees speak down mountains do
they call shouts from the top snow
coming from the bottom saying the bear
sleeps do the trees listen
to each other?

does the tree sleeping feel the bird
scratching and scratching the squirrel
pushing his sleepy back the deer
rubbing his soft horn the sun
speaking saying come awake it is spring now?

HIS HOWLING VOYAGE

now that the wind has gone
his howling voyage
down the spinning sky
now that the tree lies
still and broken on the ground
the feathered bird
still trembles in the cliff

only the sun who hid
himself behind the growling
face of the cloud
only he comes white
into the steam sky

then moving first a fox
then moving first a crow
to find the food the storm
has killed for them.

I KILL HER ENEMIES

i wear the blanket of my wife
she wears the bracelet i have made
i raised the sheep
she dug the turquoise
i teach the son she gave me
she cooks the food i gave her
my wife paints me for war
i kill her enemies

when i go on the hunt
my wife goes in my heart
when my wife stays in the hogan
i also stay in her heart

we are two
we are one.

THE JUNIPER

the juniper laughed a great laugh
the juniper shouted a great shout
the juniper stretched out his arms
and he said

i am strong

i am brave

i am beautiful

i am tall

i am wise

for have i not climbed the great mountain?
for do i not look down on firs and spruces?
for have i not lived all the winters?
for do i not see the sun first in the mornings?
for do i not feed all the so many birds?

the juniper said to me come and sit
in the only shade the mountain has
the juniper said rest beneath me
and i will tell you all the wisdom.

THERE IS A HUNGRY WATCHING

the prairie tries to eat the forest
the forest tries to eat the prairie
i see some grasses in the edge of trees
like fingers of hands claws of paws
i see some small trees in the grasses
like toes of feet hands of arms

the prairie looks at the forest
the forest looks at the prairie
the prairie does not sleep
the forest does not sleep
there is a crouching waiting between them
there is a hungry watching between them

the people of the north wish to eat my people
the people of the south wish to eat my people
my people wish to eat the north and south people

the edge of the prairie the edge of the forest
are dying there is blood along the edge
the edges of all the peoples
there is blood there are dead bodies there

will there always be war between the prairie and the forest?

will there always be war among the peoples?

I TOOK HIS SCALP

when he came over the rock
eyes like fire
mouth screaming
sweat running streams of paint
swinging the tomahawk
like a quick stone
falling from the sky

then he was dying dead
blood in the sand

i took his scalp
as i had been taught.

THE EARTH ALWAYS LIES ON HIS BACK

there is the mountain
there is the valley
there is the plain beyond
the earth is wrinkled and scarred
like my old face
the earth has had his battles
the earth has had his peace
the earth is as old
as me

after the years of travels
i rest in shade or sun
to suit the wish of the wind

i lie on the great old earth
i scratch his belly with my hand
for the earth always lies on his back
staring with his eyes of lakes
into the sky of his god.

SINGING WOLF SPEAKS

singing wolf speaks loud
singing wolf speaks courage
singing wolf speaks glory
singing wolf speaks scalps
singing wolf speaks victory
singing wolf speaks coups
singing wolf speaks pride

singing wolf speaks madness
i will not go with him

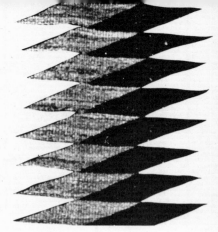

Joseph Bruchac

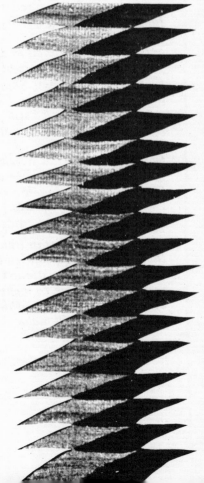

"My life has crossed many rivers since the first time when I began to think of myself as a poet. And my poems reflect the rivers and the borders that I have crossed—as well as the ones where the current is still too swift and my visa has not been granted. For me writing is that touch of the angel on your shoulder which comes when your fingers on the keys of the typewriter begin speaking in tongues.

Beyond that, however, my writing is more than a purely personal thing. My life has been enriched (or contaminated, choose the term you prefer) by the "primitive" idea of the poet as a man with a real responsibility and the idea of art for art's sake being less than the chaff in the wind which blows away and leaves the good wheat behind. So the lives and the words of men as diverse as Black Elk and Chief Joseph, an old and now blind African poet who speaks no English and is named Akpalu (may his soul have safe passage over the waters, for I feel that the touch of his hand in mine which I still feel from only a few weeks ago was the last I shall know this side of the river), Pablo Neruda, saintly Allen Ginsberg and tough and beautiful Gary Snyder, James Wright and Robert Bly and the few good teachers and good friends I have been touched by have affected me, molded the clay of my life which is still in the fire of the kiln.

When I first entered college it was as a Conservation major. I thought once that in transferring to English I had left that behind, but I can see that whatever vision is mine is that of the conservationist. I am of the earth and shall return to it. I seek to make my life and my poems a part of the whole, taking nothing without returning something in kind which will make the balance good."

WALKING

There is no loneliness outside of us
Apples in a clear glass bowl can never share our fears
The neon cafeteria lights are looking for no answers
What we call heaviness of heart
      is only iron in swinging doors

INDIAN MOUNTAIN

I.
My father and I
walk up the mountain
following an overgrown
logging road
Small trees, maple
and fire cherry saplings,
willow, birch, alder
and beech
trip our feet
and though we carry guns
we shall not shoot them
We are climbing to the top
of a mountain called Big Pisgah

II.
I stand beside
a beaver pond in a notch
between peaks
My father has gone before me
His late found love
is a memory
like the Canada geese
which landed here
gabbling far off,
sounding with distance
like a pack of hounds
My feet crush
into a fallen tree
its rotten hulk floats
in the night
alive with foxfire

I am climbing the mountain
called Little Pisgah
My hand held before me
like a lantern

III.
Jacking deer
with a light back in '34
my grandfather cruises
the old mountain road
in a battered Ford truck
fueled with hunger
But his kids ate well
that long winter
bluejays scrabbled
over the suet he hung
in the trees
and if you
could choose your end
would it be starving
life bleeding out
on grey clouded snow
or in sudden thunder
out of the night
Astonished
by the golden eye of a god

IV.
There is a stream which rises
halfway down that mountain
My father showed it to me,
place he found in a dream,
the withered spirit of an old Indian
leading him like a wisp of fog
to its banks

I shall go to that last water
when I am old
and my blood runs
like the sad Hudson river
heavy with the waste
of civilization
I shall go there
and wade into those clear ripples
where the sandy bottom
is spread with stones
which lie like the bones
of beautiful ancient animals
I shall spread my arms
in the sweet water
and go like a last wash of snow
down to the loon meadow
in the last days of April

AN AFRICAN TOWN

That was the place
where old men
left their skulls
on square plots of sand
and pebbles,
white as eggshells.

      And sometimes
in ceremonies
of rare beauty
the skulls would speak
in the tongue of the dead.

The young men, it is said,
would always listen.

When the Irish missionaries came
they danced with heavy boots
on the fragile moon-shaped bones.
They were not struck dead.

The wisest of the men
said they were dead already.

The young men smiled
and did not listen.

DRUM SONGS

I. The Drum-Maker

He owns no car
He does not wish
to go to the capital city
make laws
drink Gordon's Gin

He makes
from the living wood
in the season after rains
deep heavy drums

On the ones which are
most beautiful
he carves a human face

II. The Drummer

His clothes are shabby
A bottle of akpeteshie
and the words
you are needed tonight
for the wake-keeping of Amegah
and all other jobs are forgotten

He feels the thick pulse
throb beneath his palms
Drummers they say
must live in ragged clothes
Yet whose feet move
when a rich man says dance?

III. The Dancer

Awkward in my soul
and out of step
I am guided by them to the circle
I feel a bridge beneath me
as my feet strike the sand

and I dance
a taste in my throat sweet
as palm wine

and I wonder what god
I am being blessed by

FIRST DEER

I trailed
your guts
   a mile through snow
before my second bullet
   stopped it all.
Believe me now,
there was a boy
who fed butterflies sugar water
and kept hurt birds
in boxes in his room.

THE DOLPHIN BURIAL

The dark skin of the men
and the messenger of the Sea god
turn white with salt in the dry wind from the desert

The nets are torn
the fish scattered silver coin
on the beach and the near waves

The eyes which were deep
as the surge of tide
are closed

The men of Thunder come to the beach
a long procession of bells
and muted drums

Long ago it was seen
that the ocean people are one with us
Even the haughty steps
of the Chief Priest
betray the hesitation which marks grief

Wrapped in the shroud of blue net
that body sleek as the rushing wave
is lifted by seven men

Now, given the name
of the day of his death
he lies by the side of long past chiefs

For seven nights
let the drums compress the darkness
and spread it in throbbing tones
across Anlo

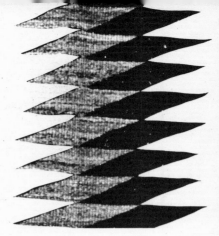

Minerva Allen

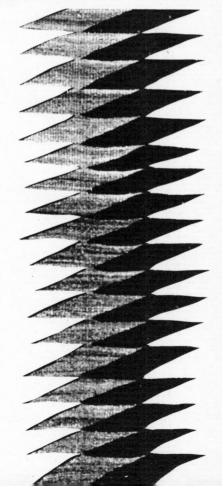

"... I am a young Assiniboine Indian woman. I live on the Fort Belknap Reservation in a village near the little Rocky Mountains. I work as a Headstart Director. I'm married to an Assiniboine Indian rancher, Tribal Council Member, and have eight children. I write poetry concerning my tribe to keep our heritage and culture."

a warm sunny day.
We traveled for suns
through rain & storm

now we reach the big water.
Horses are tired, so we rest.

My friend, our food is gone.
Who will try to find food?
I have looked up and down big water;
no sign of food anywhere. I am weary
I sleep. My friend, my stomach
talks. At last a snake.

No! My friend, do not eat the snake!
The snake is bad medicine. Sleep, my
friend, and your stomach will stop talking.

Dawn comes cold and gray. My friend,
my friend, where are you?

Here. Look down here.

Why? Why did you eat it?

This was my misfortune.
Go, my friend, I will help you across
the big water. Every time you come,
leave me something to eat and I will
lay across the big water for you to
cross on my back. Don't feel bad;
this is fate. Go and tell my people;
I have joined the snake people.

She is alone
wrinkled and gray.

Alone with clear memories.

Hard work shows its reflection on her. Tired
worn feet and hands. Holes in her teeth where
sinew was pulled. Eyes dimmed so light & dark
have no meaning. Hands tired & worn from tanning hides
and buffalo robes. She's too weary to think and hope.

Loneliness she has, for long time friends
who have gone away. Many moons & suns have passed;
time has no meaning, but life keeps marching on.

Old songs. Smell of pipe smoke.
Dry meat cooking brings the past back clear

    set aside to wait
    to meet old friends again.

Heavy clouds
hang low and gray.

The north wind is singing.
The dry leaves are rubbing against one another keeping time.

As the rain patters on the lodge
and turns to sleet,
we lie warming the soles of our feet.

Our rawhide bags are filled
with dry meat and berries.
The eatable and medicine roots
are dried and put away.
Old Man Winter is near.

You can feel his breath.
He will enclose us with snow.
The white of the weasel
and ring around the sun
        are signs.

The trees in the river bend are white.
At night we listen to the wind
rustling through the bleached trees.

The howling of the wind—
      the sadness of its song
      like an old grandfather
      mourning his son.

My time on earth has been long.
I'm old.My skin cracks as I move about
      singing sad songs;
      beating time with a drum;
      offering a pipe
      to the Sun Father
      and Earth, Mother of all.

O earth,
I go crying.
Son, where are you?
      eager to catch up with you.
Old age is a thing to bear.
It is well to die in battle young.
To be old is like walking on thin ice.

Dawn was coming.
Symbols of yellow
were shining on the hills.

Smoke was climbing out
of each lodge
like true omen.

Grandfather was up riding
from camp to camp
chanting the happenings of the day.

COME GET UP!
There's buffalo in the coulees.
Dancing and feasting tonight.

My relations,
get ready to
enjoy yourselves.
We will ride to the east.
COME!

In the dark of the night,
the stars up above
are our guide.

The moon is sleeping.
The ghost-lights dance
long streaks of light
from the earth to the sky
in the north.

Don't look my children.
It's the ghost dance.

Up north
the spirits are angry
and doing a wardance.

For suns we traveled
and then parted company.
Game was scarce. My
insides spoke.

I looked for a hollow
among the thickness pines.
I crawled tired and hungry.
The wind blew on me.
Listening to the rustling pines,
I slept.

With dawn creeping on me,
I traveled. I saw
not only a buffalo,
but a brave from another tribe.

Both arrows shot
proved true.

Enemies met
but in peace. Together
they ate and talked in sign
language.

Each took his share of meat.
They parted until they
will meet again in war.

Dog Soldier renounced life
to the One who causes things.

Dog Soldier was wounded
and left handicapped.
He felt envious.
He remained unfulfilled.

He can do the utmost damage.
He races toward the enemy.

The entire camp cries.
They lay him on his scaffold
        tying his sashes
        drums, rattles
        and medicine bundles
        to a pole.

He is left alone
to blow in the breeze
to the One above.

Returning from
scouting for meat.

Smoke hangs
low around the camp poles.
There will be fasting
and offering. The sweat lodge
will be ready.

The smell of sweetgrass
comes from the
opening of the lodge.
The pipe is offered upward
then to the ground, next
to the four winds.

Sweetgrass smokes plays
over the weapons for the hunt.
Buffalo horses are brought in
and picketed close for the run.

If the Great Spirit pities us
the hunt will be successful.
Getting ready for the hunt is
man's chief task. The buffalo
is used. It is the meaning
of life.

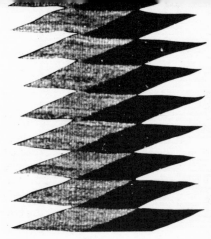

Karoniaktatie

". . . I am an Akwesasne Mohawk and have lived here all my life, been to prep school, Lenox, Mass. and that's it for education. Now starting on real learning with my people and communications—poetry editor of Akwesasne Notes. I'm not too sure about turning points in life, but Wounded Knee was something, just feeling Spirit and Blood from earth below me, the Lakotah winds . . . my writing has started to satisfy me."

Karoniaktatie means "where the sky meets the earth."

i lost the song
the song
i had
we sang
at winter forage
the song
that a lazy
crow copied
the song
i had
it was
blue
as the mountain berries
it was
red
as the pipestone
it had
deer hooves
when we walked
laughing children
when we walked
we sang
the song
i had
i lost the song
O Creation
all around
O what i did
to lose a
song
i burn
tobacco
O Creation
for the song
i had
we sang

we sing!

Karoniaktatie/67

TO MARY

sister
i have never known
your death
my birth
i wander the graveyard
searching you out
your little plot
overgrown
your cross
long lost
sister
your dreams
your shadows
your death
my birth

o sister
my sister
i love a woman
the joy
the feeling of
finding your other half
but sister
my sister
long time
i have known
your death
my birth
beside me
inside me
i will find you
a good man

between the two of us
woman
i see magic
red stones
ebony stripped
long hidden
they cry
at the touch
of an unbeliever;
i see
leather
braided
eagle plumes dancing
rainbow beads singing
turtle shell
                    &
            wolf token
you tie it
to your sash;
before us
a clay vessel
my hand/your hand
outstretched
we pour
for each other
water
from the lower world
water
sung over
by white shell grandmother;
i see
above us
clouds

Karoniaktatie/69

piled high
i sprinkle
tobacco
into the fire
smoke
curls upright
touching the
abalone sparkling
holding sky &
earth together;
i see
to the right
to the left
corn
tassels listening for
eastern whispers
(we will be);
i see
behind us
cousins
flutes in hand;
below us
red earth
murmurs
(we will be);
i see
between us
a nation.

FROM THE SEQUENCE "MEGALOMANIAC"

lookin back
walking thru the Valley of Death,
the Light Brigade lays opiated...
gazing thru massive portals
of cannon upon cannon
while the Cossacks beat the
shit out of Europe...
St. Petersburg
and the Warsaw ghetto,
ah, sweet Chicago
blow me down...

TROLL SONG

          i am growing
Look! i am growing
          i am growing
          my moccasins
          i can't fit
          my leggings
          i can't fit
          my kastoweh
          it fell off
          my hair dances
          in the wind now
naked, i am growing
yes   only naked will i grow

FROM THE SEQUENCE "CONFESSIONS OF THE GRAND MANIPULATOR"

5.

across the fields
over rotting trees & folds of waste
a walk away
blasphemy looms
grey and ugly
white
i am tired of the whiteness
i would kill the whiteness
i would bury the stench deep...
it seeps
it strangles
mother...
it seeps about me
billowing
gas...addicted Europe
gas...rampant Africa
gas...epidemic Asia
Australia never had a chance
auschwitz nebulous
Hitler is just a word now
they never really bothered me
but it seems to fit
again and again
it's boring
it's deadly

i do not want to be/ white/
i would fight
i'm tired of the translation
i would fight

again and again
sweet desperation
disillusionment
of paled genes

freedom
manic frustration
freedom is just a word now
to forget the scars

even my tears bleed...
wounded face

i have seen
the material world
i have tasted
its bitter fruit
i have feasted
& still starve
are we to end
as cattle
brother/sister animals
domesticated
continually fed
at mouldering troughs
feeding a nation
on lies & cancer
suckling mutant
cowboy fantasies
an electric prod
when yer outta place
standing
upon a hill
in a drug-induced
dream
waiting for the slaughter
waiting for the Peace

remember
the stories
of cattle in the streets
of housewives freaking at
the sight of creatures who
give life (as we know it)
to their children
perhaps they were shocked
at the sight of uncovered
motherhood
of policemen shooting
down the shuffling freedomseekers
bellowing the leader slain
others shot & prodded
so sad-eyed
but when yer outta place. . .

Karoniaktatie/75

BRIDGE POEM

VI

someone
killed a swallow
today
quite accidently
flew right into
the stone...
i mean
you never think
you'll hit one...
it fell
      into the river
went over the dam
now
the Birds
are crazy
diving
at the stone-throwers
followed them to
& from the dam
trying to clip
them   shit on
them   maybe
fly right into
their faces
pushing them
into the river
         over the dam

i mean
you never think
you'll hit one
              i mean
i'm staying
off   the bridge
          today
          ...
          i know what it's
          like
          that Cat played
          the innocent
          & died
maybe
i'll stay
off   the bridge
          for a few days

Karoniaktatie/77

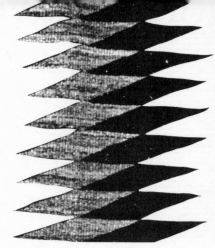

Leslie Silko

"I'm a mixed-breed Laguna Pueblo woman. If you know anything about Indian people, you'll know what this means. I grew up at Old Laguna (New Mexico) and attended BIA grade school there. Rode the bus every day 100 miles round-trip to jr. high and high school. Graduated from the U. of New Mexico in 1969 Magna Cum and Phi Beta Kappa. Moved back to the Laguna Reservation and went to law school three semesters, got divorced, quit law school, got married again. Presently I live with my husband, John Silko, in Ketchikan, Alaska, where I write fiction and poetry and he works as the supervising attorney for Alaska Legal Services.

I write because I love the stories, the feelings, the words. Occasionally, I think about innovations in style and form; such thinking doesn't get a writer very far. I find publishing a big hassle with no money coming in return and people angry all the time. But I keep trying it, like Coyote who keeps coming back for more--never quite learning his lesson."

A GERONIMO STORY

Most of the scouts were at the corrals catching their horses
and saddling up; I saw them there, busy, getting ready to
go and the feeling of excitement hit me in my stomach. I
walked faster. The dust in the first corral was so thick that
I couldn't see clearly. The horses were running in crowded
circles while the men tried to rope them. Whenever someone
threw a rope, all the horses would bolt away from it carry-
ing their heads low. I didn't see our horses. Maybe Mariano
thought that me and my uncle weren't going and he left our
horses in the pasture.

For awhile it had looked like my uncle couldn't go this time
because of his foot; he tripped over a big rock one night
when he was coming back from the toilet and he broke
some little bones in his foot. 'The sparrow bones' he called
them, and he wrapped up his foot in a wide piece of buck-
skin and wore his moccasins instead of cavalry boots. But
when Captain Pratt came to the house the night after they
got the message about Geronimo, Siteye shook his head.
"Shit," he said, "these Lagunas can't track Geronimo
without me." Captain said 'o.k.' Siteye sat there staring
out the screen door into the early evening light; then he
looked at me. "I think I'll bring my nephew along. To
saddle my horse for me." Captain nodded, and I shook
hands with him. I'd just turned 15 and I would be the
youngest man in the outfit.

The other corral was full of horses; they were standing
quietly because nobody was in there trying to catch them.
They saw me coming and backed away from me snorting
and crowding each other into the corner of the corral. I
saw Rainbow right away. My uncle's horse. A tall strong
horse that my uncle bought from a Mexican at Cubero; my
uncle has to have a big horse to carry him. The horses that
we raise at Laguna don't get as powerful as Rainbow; but
they eat less. Rainbow always ate twice as much. Like my
uncle. Siteye is a big man—tall and really big—not fat

though, big like an elk who is fast and strong—big like that. I got the lariat rope ready and stepped inside the corral;the horses crowded themselves into the corners and watched me, probably trying to figure out which one of them I was going to catch. Rainbow is easy to catch; he can't duck his head down as low as the others. He was fat and looked good. I put the bridle on him and led him out the gate, watching careful to see that one of the others didn't try to sneak out the gate behind us. It was hard to swing the saddle onto his back; Siteye's saddle is a heavy Mexican saddle—I still use it and even now it seems heavy to me.

The cinch would hardly reach around his belly; "Goddamn it horse," I told him, "don't swell up your belly for me." I led him around a little to fool him so that he would let the air out; then I tightened the cinch some more. He sighed like horses do when you cinch them up good and they know you've got them. Then when I was finished all I had to do was drop the bridle reins because this horse was specially trained to stand like he was tied up when you dropped the reins in front of him; and he would never wander away, even to eat. I petted him on the neck before I went to catch my horse; Rainbow was such a beautiful color too—dark brown with long white streaks of white on each of his sides—streaks that ran from behind his ears to the edge of his fat flanks. He looked at me with gentle eyes; that is a funny thing about horses—wild and crazy when they are loose in the corral together and so tame when they've got a saddle on them.

My horse was a little horse; he wasn't tall or stout—he was like the old-time Indian horses—that's what my father told me; the kind of horse that can run all day long and not get tired or have to eat much. Best of all he was gold colored—a dark red-gold color with a white mane and tail. The Navajos had asked $20 for him when they were only asking $12 for their other saddle horses; they wanted cash—gold or silver—no trade. But my mother had a sewing machine—one that some white lady had given her; my mother said it sewed too fast for her and it almost ran over her fingers. So we offered them this new sewing machine with silver engraved trimming on it and a wooden case; they took it and that's how I got my first horse. That day he was hard to catch; he could hide in between the bigger horses and escape my rope. By the time I managed to catch him I could hear Siteye yelling at me from the other corral "Andy," he called, "Andy where's my horse—we're ready to go."

It was almost noon when we crossed the river below the pueblo and headed southwest. Captain Pratt was up ahead and Siteye and Sousea were riding beside him; I stayed behind because I didn't want to get in anyone's way or do anything wrong. We were moving at a steady fast walk. It was late April and it wasn't too cold or too hot; a good time of year when you can travel all day without any trouble. Siteye stayed up ahead for a long time with Captain, but finally he dropped back to ride with me for awhile; maybe he saw that I was riding all by myself. He didn't speak for a long time. We were riding past Crow Mesa when he finally said something.

"We'll stop to eat pretty soon."

"Good," I said, " because I'm hungry." I looked at Siteye. His thick long hair was beginning to turn white; his thighs weren't as big as they once had been, but he's still strong, I said to myself, he's not old.

"Where are we going?" I asked him again, to make sure.

"Pie Town, north of Datil. Captain says someone there saw Apaches or something." We rode for awhile in silence. "But I don't think Geronimo is there; he's still at White Mountain."

"Did you tell Captain?"

"I told him and he agrees with me. Geronimo isn't down there. So we're going down."

"But if you already know that Geronimo isn't there," I said, "why do you go down there to look for him?" Siteye reached into his saddlepack and pulled out a paper bag full of gum drops and licorice; he took two or three pieces of candy and he handed me the bag. The paper sack rattled when I reached into it and my horse shied away from the noise. I lost my balance and I would have fallen off but Siteye saw and he grabbed my left arm to steady me. I dismounted to pick up the bag of candy; only a few pieces had spilled when it fell. I put them in my mouth and held the quivering horse with one hand and rattled the paper bag with the other. After a while he got used to the sound and he quit jumping. "He better quit that," I said to Siteye after we started again, "he can't jump every time you give me a piece of candy." Siteye shook his head. "Navajo horses. Always shie away." He paused..."It will be a beautiful journey for you. The mountains and the rivers. You've never seen them before."

"Maybe next time I come we'll find Geronimo," I said.

"Umm." That's all Siteye said. Just sort of grunted like he didn't agree with me but didn't want to talk about it either.

We stopped below Owl's Rock to eat; Captain had some of the scouts gather wood for a fire and he pulled a little tin pot out of his big leather saddle bag. He always had tea, Siteye said. No matter where they were or what kind of weather. Siteye handed me a piece of dried deer meat; he motioned with his chin towards Captain; Siteye was chewing meat. "See that," he said to me, "I admire him for that. Not like a white man at all; he has plenty of time for some tea." It was a few years later that I heard how some white people felt about Captain drinking Indian tea and being married to an Indian woman. 'Squaw man.' But back then I wondered what Siteye was talking about.

"Only one time when he couldn't have tea for lunch. When Geronimo or some Apache hit that little white settlement near the Mexican border." Siteye paused and reached for the army-issue canteen by my feet. "That was as close as the Apaches ever got. By the time we got there the people had been dead at least three days. The Apaches were 'long gone,' as people sometimes say." It was beautiful to hear Siteye talk; his words were careful and thoughtful, but they followed each other smoothly to tell a good story. He would pause to let you get a feeling for the words; and even silence was alive in his story.

"Wiped out—all of them. Women and children. Left them laying all over the place like sheep when coyotes are finished with them." He paused for a long time and carefully rewrapped the jerky in the cheese cloth and replaced it in the saddle pouch; then he rolled himself a cigarette and he licked the wheat paper slowly, using his lips and tongue.

"It smelled bad. That was the worst of it—the smell."

"What was it like?" I asked him.

"Worse than a dead dog in August," he said, "an oily smell that stuck to you like skunk odor. They even left a dead man in the well; so I had to ride 4 miles to Salado creek to take a bath and wash my clothes." He lit the cigarette that he'd just rolled and took a little puff into his mouth. "The 9th Cavalry was there. They wanted Captain to take us Scouts and get going right away." He offered me the Bull Durham pouch and the wheat papers. I took it and started making a cigarette; he watched me closely. "Too much tobacco," he said, "no wonder yours look like tamales."
I lit the cigarette and Siteye continued. 'The smell was terrible. I went over to Captain and I said "Goddamn it Captain, I have to take a bath. This smell is on me.' He was riding around with his handkerchief over his mouth and nose so he couldn't talk—he just nodded his head. Maybe he wanted to come with us, but he had to stay behind with the other officers who were watching their men dig graves. One of the officers saw us riding away and he yelled at us, but we we just kept going because we don't have to listen to white men." There was a silence like Siteye had stopped to think about it again. "When we got back one of the officers came over to me; he was angry: 'why did you go?' he yelled at me. I smiled at him and said: 'That dirty smell was all over us. It was so bad we knew the coyotes would come down from the hills tonight to carry us away—mistaking us for rotten meat.' The officer was very upset—maybe because I mentioned rotten meat, I don't know; finally he rode away and joined the other officers. By then the dead were all buried and the smell was already fading away. We started on the trail after the Apaches, and it is a good thing that scouts ride up ahead because they all smelled pretty bad—especially the soldiers who touched the dead. 'Don't get down wind from the Army,' that's what we said to each other the rest of the week, while we hunted Geronimo."

II.

We started to ride again. The sun had moved around past us and in a few more hours it would be dark. Siteye rode up front to talk to the other scouts and smoke. I watched the country we were riding into: the rocky pinon foothills high above the Acoma mesas. The trail was steep now and the trees and boulders were too close to the trail and if you didn't watch where you were going, the branches would slap your face. I had never been this far south before. This was Acoma land and nobody from Laguna would come to hunt here unless he was invited. Good hunting country.

The sun disappeared behind the great black mesa we were climbing, but below us, in the wide Acoma valley the sunlight was bright and yellow on the sandrock mesas. We were riding into the shadows and I could feel night approaching. We camped in the narrow pass that leads into the malpais country north of the Zuni mountains.

"Hobble the horses, Andy. We're still close enough that they will try to go home tonight," Siteye told me. "All four feet." So I hobbled them with each foot tied close to the other so that they could walk slowly or hop but they couldn't run. The clearing we camped in had plenty of grass but no water. In the morning there would be water when we reached the springs at Moss-Covered Rock. The horses could make it till then. We ate dried meat and flaky dry sheets of thin corn-batter bread; we all had tea with Captain. Afterwards everyone sat near the fire because winter still lingered on this high mesa where no green leaves or new grass had appeared. Siteye told me to dig a trench for us and before we laid down, I buried hot coals under dirt in the bottom of the trench; I rolled up in my blanket and I could feel the warmth beneath me. I laid there and I watched the stars for a long time. Siteye was singing a spring song to the stars; it was an old song with words about rivers and oceans in the sky. As I was falling asleep I remember the Milky Way—it was an icy snow river across the sky.

III.

The lava flow stretches for miles north to south; and the distance from east to west is difficult to see. Small pines and
pinons live in places where soil has settled on the black rock; in
these places there are grass and shrubs; rabbits and a few
deer live there. It is a dark stone ocean with waves and
ripples and deep holes. The Navajos believe that the lava is
a great pool of blood from a dangerous giant who the Twin
Brothers mortally wounded a long time ago. We rode down
the edge of the lava on a trail below the sandrock cliffs that
rise above the lava; in some places there is barely room for
two horses to pass side by side. The black rock holds the
warmth of the sun; the grass and leaves were turning green
faster than the plants and bushes of the surrounding country.

When we stopped for lunch we were still travelling along the
edge of the lava. I had never walked on it and there is something about seeing it that makes you want to walk on it—to
see how it feels under your feet and to walk in this strange
place. I was careful to stay close to the edge because I know
it is easy to lose sight of landmarks and trails. Pretty soon
Siteye came. He was walking very slowly and limping with
his broken foot. He sat down on a rock beside me. "Our
ancestors have places here," he commented as he looked
out over the miles of black rock. "In little caves they left
pottery jars full of food and water. These were places to
come when somebody was after you." He stood up and
started back slowly. "I suppose the water is all gone now,"
he said, "but the corn might still be good." When we finally
left the lava flow behind and moved into the foothills of the
Zuni mountains, Siteye looked behind us over the miles of
shining black rock. "Yes," he said, "it's a pretty good
place. I don't think Geronimo would even travel out there."

Siteye had to ride up front most of the time after we
entered the Zuni mountains; Captain didn't know the trail
and Sousea wasn't sure of it. Siteye told me later he wasn't
sure either, but he knew how to figure it out. That night we
camped in the high mountains where the pines are thick and
tall. I laid down in my blanket and watched the sky fill with

Silko/87

heavy clouds and later in the night, rain came; it was a light spring rain that came on the mountain wind. At dawn the rain was gone and I still felt dry in my blanket. Before we left, Siteye and Captain squatted in the wet mountain dirt and Siteye drew maps near their feet; he used his fore-finger to draw mountains and canyons and trees.

Later on Siteye told me "I've only been this way once before. When I was a boy. Younger than you. But in my head, when I close my eyes, I can still see the trees and the boulders and the way the trail goes. Sometimes I don't re-member the distance—things are closer or farther than I had remembered them, but the direction is right." I understood him. Since I was a child my father had taught me and Siteye had taught me to remember the way: to remember how the trees look: dead branches or crooked limbs; to look for big rocks and remember their shape and their color, and if there aren't big rocks, then little ones with pale green lichens growing on them. To know the trees and rocks all together with the mountains and sky and wildflowers. I closed my eyes and tested my vision of the trail we had traveled so far. I could see the way in my head and I had a feeling of it too— a feeling for how far the great fallen oak was from the mossy rock springs.

"Once I couldn't find the trail off Big Bead mesa. It was getting dark. I knew the place was somewhere nearby; then I saw an old gray snake crawling along a sandy wash. His rattles were yellowy brown and chipped off like an old man's toe nails." Siteye rearranged his black felt hat and cleared his throat. "I remembered him. He lived in a hole under a twisted tree at the top of the trail. The night was getting chilly because it was late September. So I figured that he was probably going back to his hole to sleep. I followed him. I was careful not to get too close—that would offend him and he might get angry and go somewhere else just to keep me away from his hole. He took me to the trail." Siteye laughed. "I was just a little kid then, and I was afraid of the dark. I ran all the way down the trail and I didn't stop until I got to my house."

IV.

By sundown we reached Pie Town. It didn't look like
Geronimo had been there. The corrals were full of cows and
sheep; no buildings had been burned. The windmill was turning slowly, catching golden reflections of the sun on the
spinning wheel. Siteye rode up front with Sousea and Captain;
they were looking for the Army that was supposed to meet us
here. I didn't see any Army horses but then I didn't see any
horses at all. Then a soldier came out of the two-story house;
he greeted Captain and they talked. The soldier pointed
towards the big arroyo behind the town.

Captain told us that they were keeping all the horses in a
big corral in the arroyo because they expected Geronimo
anytime. We laughed while we rode down the sloping path
into the wide arroyo. Siteye handed me Captain's sorrel
mare and Rainbow for me to unsaddle and feed; I filled
three gunny sack feed bags with crushed corn that I found
in the barn. I watched them eat—tossing their heads up in
the air and shaking the bags to reach the corn. They stood
still when it was all gone and I pulled the feed bags off over
their ears. I took the feed bags off the other Laguna horses;
then I tossed them all a big pile of hay. In the other half
of the big corral the Pie Town horses and Army mounts had
gathered to watch the Laguna horses eat. They watched
quietly. It was dark by the time I finished with the horses
and the others had already gone up to the big house to eat;
the shadows in the arroyo were black and deep; I walked
slowly and I heard a mourning dove calling from the tama-
rack trees.

They would have good food, I knew that. This place was
named for the good pies that one of the women could make.
I knocked on the screen door and inside I could see an old
white woman in a red checked dress; she walked with a limp.
She opened the door and pointed towards the kitchen. The
scouts were eating in there, except for Captain who was invited to eat with the white people in the dining room. I
took a big plate from the end of the table and I filled it up
with roast meat and beans; on the table there were two

plates of hot fresh bread. There was plenty of coffee, but I didn't see any pies. Siteye finished and pushed his plate aside; he poured himself another cup of coffee.

"Looks like all the white people in this area moved up here from Quemado and Datil, in case Geronimo comes—all crowded together to make their last stand." Siteye laughed at his own joke. "It was Major Littlecock who sent out the Apache alert. He says he found an Apache campsite near here. He wants us to lead him to Geronimo." Siteye shook his head. "We aren't hunting deer," he said, "we're hunting people. With deer I can say 'well, I guess I'll go to Pie Town and hunt deer' and I can probably find some around here. But with people, you must say 'I want to find these people—I wonder where they will be." Captain came in. He smiled. "Yes, we tried to tell him both of us." Siteye nodded his head. "Captain even had me talk to him and I told him in good English I said 'Major, it is so simple. Geronimo isn't even here; he's at White Mountain. They are still hunting meat,' I told him, 'meat to dry and carry with them this spring.' " Captain was sitting in the chair beside me. He brought out his tobacco and he passed it around the table; we all rolled ourselves a cigarette. For awhile nobody said anything; we all sat there smoking and resting our dinner. Finally Mariano said "Hey, where are we going to sleep tonight? How about this kitchen?" "You might eat everything," Siteye answered. "I think it will be o.k. to sleep in the kitchen," Captain said. Then Major Little-cock came in. We all stared and none of us stood up for him; Indian scouts never did that for anyone; Captain didn't stand up because he wasn't really in the Army either—only a civilian volunteer. Littlecock wasn't young; he was past 30 and his hair was falling out. He was short and pale and he kept rubbing his fingertips together. He spoke rapidly.

"I will show you the Apache camp in the morning. Then I want you to track them down and send a scout back to lead me to the place. We'll be waiting here on alert." He paused but kept his eyes on the wall above our heads. "I can understand your error concerning Geronimo's location. But we have sophisticated communications—so I couldn't expect you to be aware of Geronimo's movements." He smiled nervously; then with a great effort, he examined us. We were wearing our Indian clothes—white cotton pants, calico shirts and woven Hopi belts; Siteye had his black wide brim hat; most of us were wearing moccasins. "Weren't you men issued uniforms?" Siteye spoke. "We wear them in the winter. It's too hot for wool now." Littlecock looked at Captain. "Our Crow Indian boys preferred their uniforms," he said. There was silence; it wasn't hostile, but nobody felt like saying anything—I mean what was there to say? Crow Indian scouts like army uniforms and Laguna scouts wear them if it gets cold. Finally Littlecock moved towards the door to leave. "I was thinking the men could sleep here in the kitchen, Major. It would be more comfortable for them." Littlecock's face was pale, he moved stiffly. "I regret Captain, it isn't possible. Army regulations—civilian quarters—the women," he said, "you know what I mean, Captain. You Captain, you of course are welcome to sleep here." Littlecock smiled; he was looking at all of us. "You boys won't mind sleeping with the horses, will you."

Siteye looked intently at the Major's face and he spoke to him in Laguna: "You are the one who has use for horses at night, Major, *you* sleep with them." We all started laughing. Littlecock looked confused. "What did he say, Captain Pratt, could you translate that for me, please." His face was red and he looked angry. Captain was calm. "I'm sorry, Major, but I don't speak the Laguna language very well, I didn't catch the meaning of what Siteye said." Littlecock didn't believe him; he faced Captain squarely and spoke in a very cold voice "It is very useful to speak the Indian language fluently, Captain. I have mastered Crow and Arapaho and I was fluent in Sioux dialects before I was transferred here." He looked at Siteye and then he left the room.

We got up from the table. Siteye belched loudly and rearranged his hat. Mariano and George reached into the wood box by the stove and made little toothpicks for themselves out of the kindling chips. We walked down to the arroyo joking and laughing about sleeping out with the horses instead of inside. "Remind me not to come back to this place," Mariano said.

"I only came because they pay me," George said, "and next time they won't even be able to pay me to come here." Siteye cleared his throat. "I am only sorry that the Apaches aren't around here," he said, "I can't think of a better place to wipe out. If we see them tomorrow we'll tell them to come here first." We were all laughing and we felt good saying things like this. 'Anybody can act violently—there is nothing to it; but not every person is able to destroy his enemy with words' that's what Siteye always told me and I respect him.

We built a big fire to sit around. Captain came down later and put his little tea pot on hot coals from the fire; for a white man he could talk Laguna language pretty good and he liked to listen to the jokes and stories although he never talked much himself. And Siteye once told me that Captain didn't like to brew his Indian tea around white people; 'they don't approve of Indian tea.' Captain drank his tea slowly and he kept his eyes on the flames of the fire; a long time after he had finished the tea he stood up slowly; "sleep good" he said to us and he rolled up in his big gray Navajo blanket. Siteye rolled himself another cigarette while I covered the hot coals with sand and laid our blankets on top. Before I went to sleep I said to Siteye "You've been hunting Geronimo for a long time, haven't you. And he always gets away." "Yes," Siteye said staring up at the stars, "but I always like to think that it's us who get away."

At dawn the next day Major Littlecock took us to his Apache campsite. It was about four miles due west from Pie Town in the pine forest. The cavalry approached the area with their rifles cocked and the Major was holding his revolver. We followed them closely. "Here it is." Littlecock pointed to a corral woven with cedar branches; there was a small hearth with stones around it; that was all. Siteye and Sousea dismounted and walked around the place without stopping to examine the hearth and without once stopping to kneel down and look at the ground closely. Siteye finally stopped outside the corral and rolled himself a cigarette; he made it slowly, tapping the wheat paper gently to get just the right distribution of tobacco. I don't think I ever saw him take so long to roll a cigarette. Littlecock had dismounted and was walking back and forth in front of his horse, waiting. Siteye lit the cigarette and took two puffs of of it before he walked over to Captain; he shook his head.

"Some Mexican built himself a sheep camp here, Captain, that's all." Siteye looked at the Major to make certain he would hear. "No Geronimo here, like we said." Captain Pratt nodded his head. Littlecock mounted; he had lost and he already knew it. "Accept my apology for this inconvenience, Captain. I didn't want to take any chances." He looked at all of us; his face had a troubled, dissatisfied look; maybe he was wishing for the Sioux country up north where the land and the people were familiar to him. Siteye felt the same. "If he hadn't of killed them all off he could still be up there chasing Sioux; he might have been pretty good at it."

It was still early in the day; the forest smelled green and wet. I got off my horse to let him drink in the little stream. The water was splashing and shining in sunlight that fell through the tree-tops. I knelt on a mossy rock and felt the water. Cold water—a snow river. I closed my eyes and drank it; 'precious and rare,' I said to myself, water that I have not tasted, water that I might never taste again. The rest of the scouts were standing in the shade discussing something. Siteye walked over to me.

"We'll hunt," he said. "Good deer country down here." By noon time there were six bucks and a fat doe hanging in the trees near the stream. We ate fresh liver for lunch and afterwards I helped them bone out the meat into thin strips and Sousea salted it and strung it on a cotton line; he hung it in the sun and started to dry it. We stayed all afternoon sleeping and talking. Before the sun went down I helped Sousea put the pounds of salted meat strips into gunny sacks and tie them on the kitchen burros who hardly had anything left to carry. When we got back to Pie Town it had been dark for a long time.

In the morning the white ladies made us a big meal; we took a long time to eat and it was almost noon before we started northeast again. We went slow and we stopped early so Sousea could hang the meat out to dry for a few hours each day. When we got back to Flower Mountain I could see Laguna on the hill in the distance. "Here we are again," I said to Siteye. We stopped. Siteye turned around slowly and looked behind us at the way we had come; the canyons, the mountains, the rivers we had passed. We sat there for a long time remembering the way, the beauty of our journey. Then Siteye shook his head gently. "You know," he said, "that was a long way to go for deer hunting."

INDIAN SONG: SURVIVAL

1.
We fled north
            to escape winter
beyond pale cliffs   and
we paused to sleep by the river.

2.
Cold water   river cold from the north
I sink my body in the shallow
                sink into sand
                     and cold river water.

3.
You sleep in the branches
              of pale river willows
                  above me.
I smell you among the silver leaves, mountainlion man,
green willows aren't sweet enough to hide you.

4.
I have slept with the river
              and it is warmer than any man.
At sunrise
        I saw ice on the cattails.

5.
Mountain lion with wide yellow eyes
            you nibble moon flowers
                 while we wait.
I don't ask   why you come with me
            on desperation journey north.

6.
We are hunted for our feathers
           so we hide in spider webs
             hanging in a thin gray tree
             near the river.

Silko/95

In the night I hear music
                    song of branches
                            wide leaves scraping the moon.
7.
Green spotted frogs sing to the river
                    and I know that Simon is already waiting
                                    in the mountains.

You show me the way
                the secret path to Beyond
                        climbing higher
                                higher to blue clouds
8.   up   to the mountains.
It is a matter of time, Indian,
                    they tell me,
                        you can't sleep with the river forever;
                        smell winter and know.

9.
Above the world
            on Blue Mountain
                    I swallow black mountain dirt
while you catch hummingbirds,
                    trapping them with wildflower petals
                                    that have fallen
                            from the Milky Way.
10.
 You lay beside me in the sunlight
                    warmth around us   and
                        you ask me if I still smell winter.

Mountainforestwind travels east and I answer:
                    taste me,
                        I am the wind
                    touch me,
                        I am the lean gray deer running on
                            the edge of the rainbow.

THE TIME WE CLIMBED SNAKE MOU|

seeing good places
                for my hands
I grab the warm parts of the cliff
                and I feel the mountain as I climb.

somewhere   around here
        yellow spotted snake is sleeping
                                on his rock
                                        in the sun.

so please,
        I tell them,
                watch out,
don't step on yellow spotted snake,
                        he lives here.
                        The mountain is his.

PRAYER TO PACIFIC OCEAN

1.
I traveled to the ocean
                from my southwest land of sandrock
to moving blue water as big as the myth of origin.

2.
Pale, pale water in the yellow white-light of
    sun   floating away west where the water comes from China
The clouds that blow across the sand are white.

3.
Squat in the wet sand and speak to the ocean:
    I return to you the turquoise the red coral you sent us,
                                sister spirit of Earth.
Four round stones in my pocket   I carry back the ocean
                                to suck and to taste.

4.
Thirty thousand years ago
                Indians came riding across the ocean
                                on giant sea-turtles.
Waves were high the day that the great sea-turtles
                        waded out of the gray sundown sea.
Grandfather Turtle rolled in the sand four times
and disappeared into ocean clouds
                        swimming after the sun.

5.
And so   from that time
                        immemorial,
                                as the old people say,
Rainclouds drift from the west
                gift of the ocean to pueblo people.

LAUGHING AND LAUGHING

There was this man from Mesita. He wasn't young, but he
was seeing this woman. And she wasn't young either,
around 35 and she was married too just like him with 5
or 6 kids. Anyway, the story goes that this man's wife had
caught these two together before or maybe she had just
heard about them, I don't know. Maybe some of her
neighbors told her. Well, anyway, it was in the summer-
time after the corn was tall. That day it was hot and past
noontime and everybody was inside resting or sleeping.
And that is what these two were counting on—while
everybody else was inside resting from the heat, they
could lay down with each other out in the corn field. I
don't know whose field it was, but I guess they waited
until all the other people left their fields to eat lunch and
rest. Well, there they were, I guess, on the shady ground,
a little damp from the last weeks rain, sort of cool, maybe,
and all surrounded by the tall corn leaves that rustled a
little in the breeze. They were deep into those places that
people go when they are together like that when his wife
showed up. She didn't go by herself, she brought her two
sisters along with her. They knew what was going on and
they were just waiting to catch them together. So they
caught them. The man and that woman jumped up and
put on their clothes and all that time the wife and sisters
were standing there, silent, because they didn't have to
say anything. Then that other woman left and the man
was alone with his wife and sisters-in-law. By this time
his wife was crying and her sisters were telling her not to
cry, and the man stood there for awhile looking up at the
sky or maybe over at the red mesa behind the village, and
then he started hoeing weeds again. They were ignoring
him like he didn't matter anyway now that the other
woman was gone. So that's what happened, and everybody
was laughing and laughing when they heard about it at
Laguna, Paguate and Seama—we were all laughing about
something that happened at Mesita.

Silko/99

LOVE POEM

Rain smell comes with the wind
      out of the southwest.
Smell of sand dunes
                  tall grass glistening
in the rain.
Warm raindrops that fall easy
                this woman
the summer is born.
Smell of her breathing
            new life
small grey toads   hopping on damp red sand.
This woman
      whispering to dark wide leaves
                white moon flowers
      dripping little tracks in the sand.
Rain smell
      I am full of hunger
           deep and longing   to touch
wet tall grass, green and strong beneath.
This woman loved a man
         and she breathed to him her damp earth
song.
   I am haunted by this story   I remember it in cottonwood
                    leaves
      their fragrance in the shade.
   I remember it in the wide blue sky
      when the rain smell comes with the wind.

SLIM MAN CANYON

for John, May 1972

700 years ago
　　　　people were living here
　　　　water was running gently
　　　　and the sun was warm on pumpkin flowers.
It was 700 years ago
　　　　　　　　I remember
they were here
　　　　　　deep in this canyon
　　　　　　with sandstone walls rising high above them.
The rock, the silence, tall sky and flowing water
　　　　　　sunshine through cottonwood leaves
　　　　　　the willow smell in the wind
　　　　　　　　　　　　700 years ago.

The rhythm,
　　　　the horses' feet, moving strong through
　　　　　　　　white deep sand.
Where I come from is like this
　　　　the warmth, the fragrance, the silence.
Blue sky and rainclouds in the distance
　　　　we ride together
past the cliffs with the stories
　　　　　　　　the songs painted on rocks . . . .
　　　　There was a man who loved a woman
　　　　seven hundred years ago.

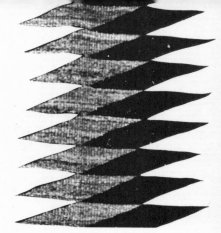

Winston Mason

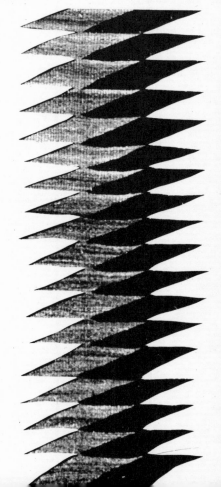

Winston Mason works with his wife in poetry, crafts and visual arts. We lost contact with him two years ago—at that time he was living in Morence, Arizona.

THE RAVEN

The raven
is stealing your corn
old mother.
The raven
with his shifty black
eyes,
with his shiny black
beak.
The raven, old mother
is stealing your corn.

"JUST A MINUTE"

"Just a minute,"
You said.
Then took the rest
of my life!

SUICIDE

My brother,
I grieve for you.
let us not be angry
for it is done.
You were gross.
You were unmannerly.
You wronged me greatly.
My brother.
It is done.
Ho! I take leave.

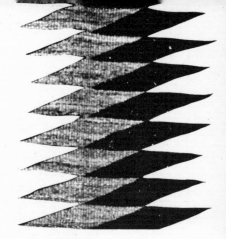

Duane Niatum

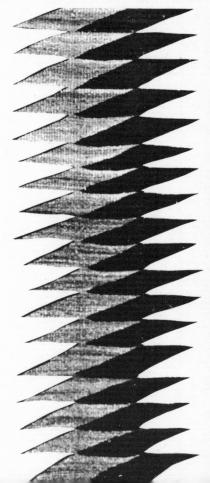

*"For some time, I have recognized my debt to my Indian
ancestry. Anyone familiar with my work will see this is
perhaps all too obvious. So, because this debt goes back
to the soil of my birth, I had always intended to write a
small book or books devoted totally to Indian themes,
spirits, visions. If my Indian Grandfather and Great-uncle
taught me nothing else, they taught me to humble my soul
before the spiritual reality of things. Andrew Joe, of the
Skagit Tribe, Washington, pretty much summed up the
Native American sensibility with the following: "When
we can understand animals, we will know the change is
halfway. When we can talk to the forest, we will know
that the change has come." Therefore, many of the poems
deal with that dimension, style of being and seeing that
suggests you live with mud on your shoes, ride out the
flights of white owl in your sleep."*

HOMAGE TO CHAGALL

1.
The candle takes the first desperate leap
through the window, flaming a rainbow
to the dark valley on the moon.

A weary juggler, in the corner, reflects on this;
decides to tumble inside the blue cow's
crystal ball, seven songs,

circling night and day. He is joyous,
and no one thinks this strange; besides, the town
has stopped the rage for foreign scrolls,

blood drying in the footprints of the goat.
Feathering the burning bush with hens,
the synagogue mosaic trades light for Spring rain.

Sleepy children on their way to school see
the bearded violinist stranding music on the poplar trees;
laughing, the green rabbi puns the Czar

in Hebrew: for decades, police have been seen
rolling off the ghetto wall like dice.

2.
And his love for woman is a peacock's dance at sunset.
Like Redon, Monet, Picasso, he masters
her lean curves along the body of the dream,

where Eros hails the painter and magician.
After catching the blossom
from the "Sun At Poros," the world turns

our bodies into reeds, our eyes into nomads.

1.
You sat with a bottle of beer in one hand,
And a steaming mussel in the other,
Chanting in the summer evening
The story of Kwatee, the Changer.
Your grandchildren huddled,
Awed by your heavy-lumbered frame
And demonic shadow painted in the sand by fire.
When your laughter cracked in pine logs
That smelled of kelp and seaweed,
We saw the story surface like a whale.

Twelve salmon harvests have passed
Since I last saw fishnets hanging through winter
Across the common stream.
What frost deep afternoon was it
When you pantomimed the legend of black elk
Who was caught only in dreams;
And the Chinook salmon held in a net,
And because of his bronze eyes and flapping defiance,
You threw him to the sea?
And when did the taste for the whale hunt
Darken to nothing more than myth?

One morning after we tossed feast bones
Back to the Herring People, we heard
You shout down the ravens,
Falling on a heap of crab shells.

Today, forest flowers and vines
Cover your home, and the animals of stone
You carved to your front door
Mirror dreams of your children's children.
What are blue forests without you, Granduncle?
Who else but your brother or sister can see
The forest breathe when the woodpecker is silent?

How long before the village grew solemn
As ashes   did you begin to die?
Was it on the reservation?
After the death of your son, or your brother?
Now your children lie stripped down
To their hides, charred saplings of cedar,
Old roots in soil of many seasons.

2.
In the twilight of Thunderbird,
I will chant to Mount Memp-ch-ton
From the yellow shades of fern as my granduncle
Did before they returned him to oyster shells
And sand, salted bones for crabs and fish.

I see him as he waved to his grandchildren
In the amber stone silence,
Watching salmon fin dark rapids of sapphire
To spawning beds in Ho-had-hun creeks.
Under thick windows of fern,
On the mountain near his father's grave,
He listened to pacific seas pound tribute
To villages of whalers and hunters,
Slowly closing his eyes to meet
The glacier's light to the cave.

As brother to the chickadee and wolf,
Rain soaked and restless,
I turn to the forests of Klallam,
In honor of my great-uncle, Joseph Patsey,
Elder to the hawk and sparrow.

Mount Memp-ch-ton is what the Klallam Tribe calls
Mt. Olympus.

Ho-had-hun is what the Nisquallys and other Olympic
Peninsula Tribes call the Olympic Mountains.

CHIEF LESCHI OF THE NISQUALLIES

He awoke this morning from a strange dream—
Thunderbird wept for him in the blizzard.
Holding him in their circle, Nisqually women
turn to the river, dance to its song.

He burned in the forest like a red cedar,
his arms fanning blue flames toward
the white men claiming the camas valley
for their pigs and fowl.
Musing over wolf's tracks vanishing in snow,
the memory of his wives and children
keeps him mute. Flickering in the dawn fires,
his faith grows roots, tricks the soldiers
like a fawn, sleeping black as the brush.

They laugh at his fate, frozen as a bat
against his throat. Still, death will take
him only to his father's longhouse,
past the flaming rainbow door. These bars
hold but his tired body; he will eat little
and speak less before he hangs.

OLD TILLICUM

for my mother's father, Francis Patsey

A timber blue haze dissolves
On chokecherry leaves,
Pebbles turn like fish in the current,
And a buck hoofs the earth
Through the black secrets of the brush.
The sky, lifting my smoked salmon frame
Over the camas meadow, the willows,
Echoes the songs our river people sang.

And old Klallam, I sit with my grandson
and hear, from the fern-shadowed distance
Elwha's movement to the sea.
I wait patiently for the dream spirit to chant,
Warm the blue-green awkwardness of youth,
Flush my grandchild's cheek
With spruce light, toss
My brittle bones to the dark.
Memp-ch-ton, mirrored in the Elwha rapids,
Magnified by the falling sun,
Dwarfs our village, rooted in raven's thunder.

Pitch dry with age, I see my grandson
Start the long journey
Down into the clearing of his manhood,
The thought of hunting seal,
Netting salmon, pulling him on like the tide,
Once frightened of the surf's crack
Below the circle of pine,
He now disappears happily past
The canyon of the mountain's hide,
A fox running in his shadow.

Muting the sun and the silence
Of a roosting pheasant,
The ridge across the ravine remembers
The brothers entering the circle,
Their eyes dancing in the cedar fires.
Slowly, like a forgotten totem
The moon drifts full height across the sky,
A crow returning to its birth.
Dawn sits beneath the white sea
Like O-le-man sleeping through Spring.

As Grandfather, I rise
Too late to walk with my grandson.

Tillicum, friend; *Elwha,* Klallam River; *Memp-ch-ton,*
Klallam for Mt. Olympus; *O-le-man,* strong one, old man,
chief.

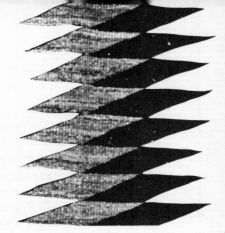

S. Roberto Sandoval

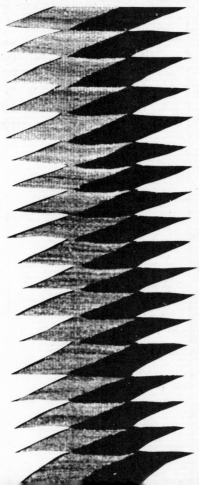

S. Roberto Sandoval . . . is a Genízaro (word designates non-Pueblo and Pueblo Indians adopting a Hispanic life-style and/or raised in a Hispanic life-style.) He was born in Taos, N.M. in 1950 and now lives in Sante Fe, N.M.

"With Grandmothers living and my only Grandfather died 1968. Great-grandmother Santus Olivas was a plains captiva (captive) in Spanish homes passed from house to house till she was old enough to marry and build her own house. She built two adobe houses by herself and delivered many babies and was a médica (healer). She had two daughters and a son. Grandma Dominga Trujillo was related to Archuletas in Taos Pueblo but she says her relatives have died out. This was my father's mother.

Lots of information was secret except for church records because of the feeling at that time for Plains people who raided and took captives and were taken captive and raided in return by peoples of Northern New Mexico.

I am of what is before I came to life. And this is all I have to say of my self at this time."

POTS

Rings
with broken lines,
unconnected curves
showing paths
that take a
man
from his house to
a water pot
center
and lets him
find his way
among his father's fingers.

Windless night with clear stars,
my face is dry and drawn tight
with this cold and I
can not rest.

Twin apples sitting on a white
mountain,
I reach for one and eat it
I grow hungry, so hungry
I awake and touch my woman's shoulder

Old friends I haven't seen
for a year thinking about
them out in Tohatchi
New Mexico
now that I'm hungry
and that damn noise
of cities
I love that dry
biting brilliant clear land
with wind always

THE WIND NEVER STOPS HERE
IN THE FALL

No clouds, the sun
making mesas
sharp in the distance
colors of earth
shine from them
wind making only
those damn
government built houses
tremble.

Going to the place where
my spirit feels strong

I looked at the mountain
whose spirit was not there
wind cried through
trees that were not there

I called for bear, lobo,
coyote, mountain lion

There are none there
                    said
an old man whose
old grey
braids grew to
dying earth.

The
pot's heart
decorating a bell
ceramic noise maker
hanging in that shop
tourist shop design
pulled from the crook of
dead man's arms
bones buried
pretty pot
that heart on a
bell.

TOUCHING ON A MOUNTAIN TOP

Two dogs waiting under a
little tree bent
telling how many

winds have blown here
rocks speaking the names
of men dead who once

touched their woman,
feeling you close, Marie
speaks of sky and earth.

Speaks a tongue
I guess
is the way to
say
it
speaks and feels
things and sees things
by his tongue or
language I guess a bigger
word for
it
language without alfabet
no pen
no paper
no black lines in your mouth
and heart
I can't say
it.